P9-DGW-423

TREASURES FROM THE PAST

TREASURES FROM EGYPT

David & Patricia Armentrout

The Rourke Book Company, Inc.
Vero Beach, Florida 32964

j932
ARM

© 2001 The Rourke Book Company, Inc.
All rights reserved. No part of this book may be reproduced or utilized
in any form or by any means, electronic or mechanical including photocopying, recording, or by any
information storage and retrieval system without permission in writing from the publisher.

PHOTO CREDITS:
©Susan Alworth: pages 16, 19, 20, 26, 29, 37, 41, 42; ©Al Michaud: pages 11, 15, 18, 27, 30; ©Galyn C.
Hammond: pages 23, 32, 33; ©Elwin Trump: pages 6, 24; ©Corel Corporation: cover; ©Artville, LLC.:
page 4

PRODUCED & DESIGNED by East Coast Studios
eastcoaststudios.com

EDITORIAL SERVICES:
Pamela Schroeder

Library of Congress Cataloging-in-Publication Data

Armentrout, David, 1962-
    Egypt / David and Patricia Armentrout.
        p. cm. — (Treasures from the past)
    Includes bibliographical references and index.
    ISBN 1-55916-289-9
    1. Egypt—Antiquities—Juvenile literature. 2. Egypt—Civilization—To 332 B.C.—Juvenile literature. [1. Egypt—
Antiquities. 2. Archaeology.] I. Armentrout, Patricia, 1960- II. Title. III. Treasures from the past (Vero Beach, Fla.)

DT60 .A8 2000
932—dc21

                                                                                        00–029074

Printed in the USA

TABLE OF CONTENTS

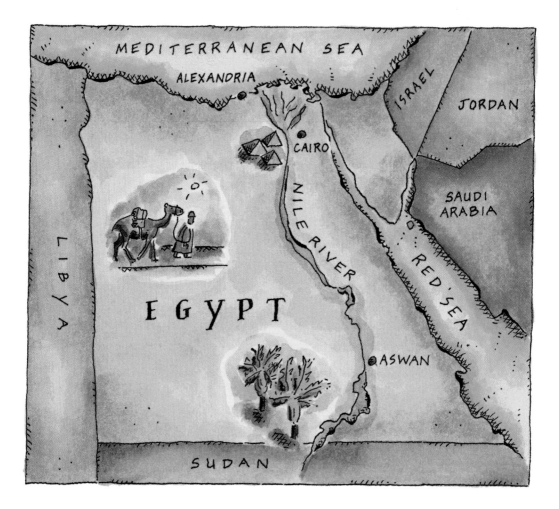

4

CHAPTER 1

LEARNING ABOUT THE PAST

We can't go back in time, but our imagination can take us to just about any place, in the future or in the past. Books help us do the same thing. You may have read stories about times long ago. They tell us what it was like to live in the past. Reading a book, you can go back to the American Revolution during the 1700s. You can read about a French explorer named LaSalle. He traveled on the Mississippi River before the revolution. There are even stories about the Vikings, who lived 1,000 years ago.

It's fun to read about the past and to imagine what it was like to live back then. Can you imagine what life was like 2, 3, or even 4,000 years ago? That's the time of ancient **civilizations**. How do we learn about the way people lived in ancient times? One way is through **archaeology**.

Archaeology is a science. It is the study of past human life. A person who practices archaeology is an archaeologist. An archaeologist's work is an investigation. Like detectives, archaeologists search for clues. They piece clues together, hoping to uncover the mysteries of the past.

People can buy fruit and vegetables in Cairo's outdoor markets.

TIMELINE

3000 – 2180 BC	The Old Kingdom.
2700 BC	The Step Pyramid is built for King Djoser.
2550 BC	The Great Pyramid is built for King Khufu.
2400 BC	Egyptians use papyrus.
2180 – 1570 BC	The Middle Kingdom Egypt is ruled by foreign Kings from Palestine—the area now known as Israel and Jordan.
1570 – 1085 BC	The New Kingdom.
1570 BC	Temples are built at Karnak and Luxor.
1512 BC	The first pharaoh is buried in the Valley of the Kings.
1304 BC	Ramses II rules Egypt. Temples at Abu Simbel are built.
332 BC	Alexandria, Egypt's second largest city, is founded by Alexander the Great.
200 BC	Dating of the Rosetta Stone.
100 BC	Cleopatra rules Egypt.
31 BC	Egypt is ruled by the Roman Empire.
AD 600	Cairo is founded.

Archaeologists explore human cultures from 100 years ago to more than 1 million years ago. They use special tools and equipment. They do research. They study remains, or **artifacts**. They record information. Archaeologists do all this to learn about life long ago.

An artifact is anything made by humans. A stone tool, like an arrow point, is an artifact. Pottery, pieces of cloth, and jewelry are all artifacts. Just imagine an archaeologist 1,000 years from now studying our time. He or she might find artifacts like a bicycle, a CD player, or your school books. Even your favorite baseball cards could someday become artifacts—treasures from the past!

Archaeology is divided into time periods. Not all archaeologists study the same period in time. Some study prehistoric time periods. Prehistoric, or prehistory, means the time before people used writing. Other archaeologists study more recent time periods.

Archaeology is divided into subjects, too. Classical archaeology is the study of ancient Greece and Rome. The study of ancient Egyptian civilizations is called **Egyptology**.

Sometimes archaeologists make their own artifacts to help them understand how true artifacts were made.

CHAPTER 2

EGYPTOLOGY

People have been interested in ancient Egyptian art and artifacts since the Middle Ages. The Middle Ages were between 500 and 1500. Explorers of that time were more like treasure hunters. They were looking for valuable objects. It's true the explorers were interested in the pyramid tombs. However, they raided the tombs for treasure. They didn't stop to learn about the civilizations that built them. The treasure hunters took the artifacts back to their homelands and traded them for money.

Treasure hunters were only interested in finding valuable objects. They did not worry about the way they treated the **dig site**. Treasure hunters often destroyed some artifacts to get to others. Most did not make notes and could not explain where they found the objects.

Modern methods of archaeology began about 200 years ago. This is when many European collectors and students traveled to Egypt to study its past. They kept careful records about a site's location. They studied artifacts and structures in detail. Archaeologists labeled all the objects that they took. Scientists tried to date artifacts, or find out when they were made. From the clues they collected, they were able to answer some important questions about ancient Egyptian life.

Ancient Egypt

Egypt is located in the northeast corner of Africa. Its most populated area is the city of Cairo *(KY roh),* Egypt's capital. In ancient times, that area was a busy, growing Egyptian civilization. Ancient Egyptians lived there because of the Nile River.

Egyptians lived on the rich, fertile soil surrounding the Nile. They farmed the soil for crops, and farmers brought their animals to the river to drink.

The Rosetta Stone was carved about 200 BC. It shows three kinds of ancient writing.

The Nile provided food and water for the Egyptians, too. Egyptians used **papyrus** boats for fishing. They used other, stronger, timber boats to travel. Small cargo boats carried grain, and larger ships carried kings and other important people. Because Egypt is such a huge, dry desert land, Egyptians believed the Nile River was "a gift."

How do we know that ancient Egyptians counted on the Nile? Archaeologists and other scientists have worked together and studied artifacts to learn what life must have been like in ancient Egypt. A 3,000-year-old fishing net is just one clue that tells us ancient Egyptians sailed and fished the Nile.

Egyptologists study the writings and language of a civilization, too. The Rosetta Stone, found by accident in 1799, is a perfect example of an artifact showing language. The stone shows three kinds of writing—one Greek and two Egyptian. From this artifact, archaeologists learned to use the ancient Egyptian way of writing, made up of **hieroglyphs**.

DIG SITES

Most people from ancient civilizations lived above ground, as we do today. Why, then, do archaeologists find things below ground? One reason is that people buried things. Just like we bury trash in landfills, people long ago buried their trash. Just like we bury our dead, ancient people buried their dead, too. However, it's not just the dead or trash that is uncovered by archaeologists. They also find valuables like gold and jewelry.

Another reason archaeologists find artifacts underground is because of a natural disaster like a flood, a sand storm, or volcanic eruption. These disasters can cover objects and even entire cities. Weather, soil **erosion**, and the **decay** of plants and animals over hundreds and even thousands of years cause new layers of earth to cover old layers. Archaeologists remove the soil, layer by layer, and find hidden treasures from the past.

Where do archaeologists dig? Archaeologists don't always know where to dig. They have to do some research first. Old maps, coins, and other papers can provide clues. They often give dates or name places, like rivers or mountains. Clues like these help in the investigation.

Sometimes it is easy to begin a search for clues. Archaeologists often look near the remains of ancient structures like the pyramids. They also mark sites where an artifact is found, even if by accident. For example, a farmer may find pottery pieces while plowing a field. The pottery could be **evidence** of a past civilization.

This stone pharaoh dates back to 3000 BC.

Parts of the Great Sphinx are being rebuilt by archaeologists.

Once a site has been chosen, work begins. First a fixed point of height is decided. Then all other measurements are based on that fixed point.

Many tools are used at a dig site. Two important tools are a tape measure and **plumb bob**. They are used for plotting, or mapping, and measuring the site. It's very important that careful records are kept during each stage of the dig.

Other tools include hand pick axes, trowels, brushes, and small dental picks. When an artifact is discovered, these tools help scientists carefully remove the soil so the object will not be harmed.

After an archaeologist finds an artifact, **data** collection begins. Scientists number the artifact, record the exact location where it was found, write a description of the artifact, make a sketch, and even take pictures of the artifact and dig site.

Aerial photography helps archaeologists see the "big picture." It's easy for archaeologists to spot patterns on the ground, like burial mounds or trenches.

However, the job doesn't stop there. After collecting data, archaeologists use **chronology** to date the artifacts. Chronology is a science that measures time and dates events. Chronology puts events into the order in which they happened. Scientists who use chronology are able to tell us about when the Egyptian pyramids where built.

Temple wall paintings show Egyptian art and picture symbols called hieroglyphs.

This gold mask covered the face of King Tutankhamun's mummy.

Visitors crowd the ruins at Karnak. Karnak has many ancient temples that spread over 120 acres (48 ha).

CHAPTER 4

EGYPTIAN PYRAMIDS

Archaeologists have learned how Egyptians lived thousands of years ago by putting together clues found in and around the pyramids.

Egyptian pyramids are named for their pyramid shape. The triangle side of a pyramid is called the face. The four faces of a pyramid meet at a point at the top. Pyramids can have a three-sided base, or bottom. However, the Egyptian pyramids have a square base and are called square pyramids.

The pyramids were built from about 2700 BC to 1000 BC. That makes the first pyramid more than 4,500 years old! Did ancient Egyptians know these huge structures would last such a long time? What were pyramids used for? The pyramids were built by Egyptians for their **pharaoh**, or king. Pyramids were used as burial monuments—a final resting place for a king's body.

It took years to build a pyramid. After a king chose a site for his monument, the building began. It took the efforts of designers, sculptors, stonecutters, and other laborers to construct the pyramid. Different kinds of stone were used including limestone, granite, and sandstone. Some stone had to be **quarried** far away from the pyramid site. It came from the other side of the Nile or up river. Boats played a major role in pyramid construction. They carried blocks of stone to the pyramid by way of the Nile River. Carvings inside some tombs show boats carrying huge stone blocks. Egyptologists have found stone cutting tools, like chisels and mallets, in and around the pyramids.

This huge stone carving is of Ramses II. He ruled Egypt from 1304 – 1237 BC.

Each stone block used to build the Great Pyramid weighs over two tons.

A major construction project today needs heavy equipment like excavators, bulldozers, and cranes. We can only imagine how the ancient Egyptians built the pyramids without modern machines. Experts have some ideas about how it was done. Most agree the huge stone blocks were dragged on wooden sleds up a long ramp. The ramp was made longer as the pyramid grew taller.

The Oldest Pyramid

The first Egyptian pyramid was built around 2700 BC for pharaoh Djoser *(ZHO ser)*. The pyramid is located at Saqqara *(suh KAHR uh)* near Cairo. Djoser's pyramid is a step pyramid, the first of its kind. It has six steps built on top of each other. Each step is a flat-topped building with sloped sides. The steps were constructed out of stones that were laid like bricks. Fine limestone covers the steps to make a smooth surface. The final height of the pyramid reached 198 feet (60m).

It was custom to **bless** the foundation of a pyramid before laying the first brick.

The Step Pyramid is part of a big complex that was designed by **architect** Imhotep. The Step Pyramid complex is a rectangular area that has several courtyards, chapels, and other rooms. The pyramid sits at one end of the complex. Djoser's burial chamber lies under the pyramid. Underground passages and Djoser's burial chamber were lined with blue tiles. A life-sized statue of Djoser was found in the tomb chamber.

The Step Pyramid was built in 2700 BC. Parts of the pyramid complex have been rebuilt.

*S*tone was taken from the outside of the Giza pyramids during
the 10th century AD. It was used to build other buildings in nearby Cairo.

French architect and Egyptologist Jean-Philippe Lauer spent years reconstructing the Step Pyramid complex. His work began in 1926. During reconstruction, huge stone columns had to be uncovered from the desert sand.

The complex is surrounded by a wall measuring 1,800 ft (550 m) long by 900 ft (275 m) wide. The wall appears to have 15 doors. However, only one door opens. Trick passageways and false doors and rooms are all over the complex. Experts feel the Djoser complex was a model of the royal palace at Memphis, Egypt. Was the royal tomb designed like a palace so Djoser could live as a king, even after his death?

The Great Pyramid at Giza

The largest pyramid in Egypt is named the Great Pyramid. The Great Pyramid is located at Giza *(GEE zuh),* Egypt. Giza is home to three major pyramids and several smaller pyramids.

The Great Pyramid was built around 2550 BC for King Khufu *(KOO foo).* The Great Pyramid stands 481 ft (147 m) high. It has a square base that is about 755 ft (230 m) at each side. We can't count all the stone blocks that make up the structure, but scientists believe there are more than 2 million limestone blocks, each weighing 2½ tons! Experts say it took about 20 years to build this ancient wonder of the world.

This pyramid was once covered with smooth limestone.

Sphinxes line the road between the Luxor and Karnak Temples.

The two other major pyramids at Giza are the Khafra *(KAH fruh)* pyramid and the Menkaura *(men KOO ray)* pyramid. King Khafra's pyramid, the center pyramid, was built around 2520 BC. Khafra was a son of Khufu. Khafra built his pyramid on higher ground than the Great Pyramid. It looks taller than his father's, but Khafra's pyramid is 9 feet (3m) shorter. King Menkaura built his pyramid around 2490 BC. Menkaura is believed to be Khafra's son. His pyramid is the smallest. It stands 218 feet (66m) high.

There are seven smaller pyramids surrounding the three major ones. The smaller pyramids are "queens" pyramids. However, the pharaohs' wives were not always buried beneath them. The most famous structure outside the pyramids is the Great **Sphinx**. The Great Sphinx is a rock structure that has a body of a lion and a head of a King (most likely King Khafra). The Great Sphinx looks east and seems to guard Khafra's pyramid. Scientists think King Khafra built the Sphinx to do just that.

The Sphinx used to be buried up to its neck in sand. Many attempts have been made to clear the sand away. A recent clearing in 1905 revealed paws 50 feet (15 m) long. The total length is 150 ft (45 m).

The outside layer of the Giza pyramids has an uneven brick surface. That is because the smooth outer layer of stone was removed and used for other buildings in Egypt. Stealing limestone from the pyramids was easier than cutting new stone blocks. Some of the outer limestone can be seen at the top of the center pyramid.

The Great Sphinx guards King Khafra's pyramid. Some people believe its nose is missing because Turkish soldiers used it for target practice.

This passageway leads to a dig site near the Giza pyramids.

Inside Pyramids

What's inside the pyramids? Egyptian pyramids are full of passageways and rooms. The Great Pyramid has a long passageway that leads from the entrance to an underground chamber. Another long passage leads upward from the entrance to the Grand Gallery, and then on to the King's Chamber. The King's Chamber is Khufu's final resting place. The chamber is lined in granite and has a roof made of nine stone slabs that weigh 50 tons each.

Khafra's pyramid was explored in 1818 by Giovanni Belzoni. He entered the king's burial chamber but found no signs of the great pharaoh. The **sarcophagus**, a stone coffin, was empty and no treasure was found. The burial chamber had been robbed by treasure hunters.

Most of the pyramids of Egypt had been robbed well before the 1800s. Archaeologists used the few treasures that were found, and the drawings and writings on the walls, to piece together the lives of the great pharaohs and those who built their tombs.

TOMBS AND TEMPLES

Cliff-side Tombs

A royal burial site called the Valley of the Kings lies in southern Egypt. It is located on the west bank of the Nile across from Luxor *(LUHK sohr)*—the ancient city Thebes. The Valley of the Kings is the final resting place chosen by most rulers of the New Kingdom. The Egyptian New Kingdom lasted from about 1570 BC to 1070 BC.

Rulers of the New Kingdom did not build huge stone pyramids in the flood plains of the Nile. These pharaohs chose a valley protected by high rock cliffs. Over 60 tombs lie deep in the rock cliffs. The Valley is in the shadow of a pyramid-shaped mountain called The Horn.

The first tomb discovered in the Valley belongs to King Seti *(SEE tee)* I. His tomb has a burial chamber decorated with beautiful art work. It has the longest burial chamber of all the tombs.

The last tomb discovered was that of King Tutankhamun *(toot ahng KAH men)*. His tomb was hidden by pieces of rock from the carvings of another king's tomb. King Tutankhamun is not known for his great reign, but for his tomb. Unlike most tombs, King Tutankhamun's had not been robbed. The tomb was discovered in 1922 by Howard Carter. Imagine how Carter must have felt when he saw that Tut's tomb was not robbed of all its treasures. Many gold items, such as weapons, jewelry, furniture, and musical instruments, were found in the tomb—over 5,000 items in all.

*V*isitors walk to the entrance of the tombs of Ramses IV
and Tutankhamun at the Valley of the Kings.

King Tutankhamun's **mummy** was found in his tomb in a solid gold coffin, the third coffin in a nest of coffins. The face of Tut's mummy was protected by a beautiful gold mask. Egyptians believed that when the spirit of the king returned to his tomb in the afterlife, he would be able to find his mummy by the decorated mask. The famous gold mask is on display in the Cairo Museum.

Temples

A temple is a large building used to worship a god or goddess. Pharaohs who built pyramid tombs also built temples. These temples were used to mummify the king and as a place of worship.

Pharaohs of the Middle and New Kingdoms also built temples. Two temples, the Luxor Temple and the Temple of Karnak *(KAHR nak),* are the most famous. The temples sit about one mile apart. At one time, though, they were joined by rows of stone sphinxes. The sphinxes' job was to guard the temple gates. You can see what's left of the sphinxes outside the Luxor Temple.

ANCIENT EGYPTIAN SOCIETY

Today we need people to do many different jobs. Bakers, tailors, potters, fishermen, priests, writers, doctors, and even rulers work in our major cities. Ancient Egyptians held many of these same jobs.

Egyptian rulers and their families lived like kings. Their homes were grand palaces built of only the finest stone. The royal family wore the most beautiful clothes woven from the finest materials. They ate only the best food made by servants.

The children of the king and queen had responsibilities that the other children did not have. A young prince had to learn how to be king. This meant hours of training. It could not have been much fun learning how to be king when other kids were playing games.

Priests were among the most important people in ancient Egypt. Although the king was the high priest, other priests carried out daily jobs. Priests cared for the temple property and treasures and took part in some ceremonies.

Scribes were also among the most important Egyptians. Scribes were well educated. They knew how to write with hieroglyphs, or picture writing. More than 700 symbols were used in hieroglyphs. It was very difficult to learn. Scribes would write on scrolls, in books, and decorate art, tombs, and other buildings.

Ancient Egyptian civilizations had fishermen, hunters, and farmers, too. Farmers counted on the Nile to flood each year to enrich the soil. Crops grew best in the soil surrounding the river, not in the sandy desert. Most of the food came from farming the land, not from hunting. The pharaoh and his men hunted for sport. The Nile supplied Egyptians with plenty of fish caught with hooks, nets, and harpoons. Harpoons were also used to hunt hippo in the river. Too many hippopotamuses caused problems with boats and the crops off shore.

The Nile River has been used for fishing, farming, and transportation for thousands of years.

*These picture symbols can be seen in the Temple of Horus in Edfu.
Horus was an ancient Egyptian sun god.*

Egyptians lived in homes made of mud bricks. They carried out everyday jobs, such as making meals and cleaning clothes, as we do today. Children enjoyed toys and games. Adults held jobs. Carpenters made furniture and carved statues using the same types of tools we use today. Doctors practiced medicine, sometimes with magic spells. This was how ancient Egyptians treated pain and disease. After all the work was done, ancient Egyptians still found time for fun. They often enjoyed song and dance.

Ancient civilizations are very much like modern ones in many ways. Archaeology is a wonderful science that teaches us how civilizations that are separated by thousands of years can be alike and how they are different.

PLACES AND NAMES PRONUNCIATION GUIDE

Places:

Cairo   *(KY roh)*

Giza   *(GEE zuh)*

Karnak   *(KAHR nak)*

Luxor   *(LUHK sohr)*

Saqqara   *(suh KAHR uh)*

People:

Djoser   *(ZHO ser)*

Khafra   *(KAH fruh)*

Khufu   *(KOO foo)*

Menkaura   *(men KOO ray)*

Seti I   *(SEE tee)*

Tutankhamun   *(toot ahng KAH men)*

GLOSSARY

archaeology (AR kee AHL uh jee) — the study of past human life by studying artifacts left by ancient people

architect (AR kih tekt) — a person who plans and watches over the way buildings are constructed

artifacts (ART eh fakts) — objects made or changed by humans

bless (BLES) — to make sacred by saying religious words or prayers

chronology (kreh NAHL uh jee) — a science that deals with measuring time and dating events

civilizations (SIV eh leh ZAY shunz) — advanced or high levels of cultural development

data (DAT eh) — factual information

decay (di KAY) — to break down or decline from a healthy condition

dig site (DIG SITE) — a place where excavation takes place

Egyptology (ee jip TAHL uh jee) — the study of ancient Egyptian civilizations

erosion (i ROE zhen) — the process of slowly rotting away or being destroyed

GLOSSARY

evidence (EV e dens) — anything that can be used as proof

hieroglyphs (HIGH reh GLIFS) — symbols used in a writing system

mummy (MUM ee) — a body preserved and prepared for burial

pharaoh (FAIR roe) — a ruler of ancient Egypt

quarried (KWOR eed) — dug from an open area to get building stone

papyrus (peh PIE res) — a tall grassy plant used to make paper

plumb bob (PLUM BOB) — a tool used to find an exact vertical measurement

sarcophagus (sar KAHF eh ges) — a large stone coffin

sphinx (sfinks) — a stone structure with a human head and a lion's body

FURTHER READING

The Young Oxford Book of Archaeology, ©1997 Norah Moloney, Oxford University Press, NY

Ancient Egyptian Pharaohs, ©1998 Jo Forty, PRC Publishing Ltd., London

Archeology, Eyewitness Books, ©1994 Dr. Jane McIntosh, Alfred A. Knopf, Inc., NY

Ancient Egypt, Eyewitness Books, ©1990 George Hart, Alfred A. Knopf, Inc., NY

Pyramid, Eyewitness Books, ©1994 James Putnam, Alfred A. Knopf, Inc., NY

Archaeology Magazine
  www.archaeology.org/

The Seven Wonders: The Great Pyramid of Giza
  www.//ce.eng.usf.edu/pharos/wonders/pyramid.html

INDEX